# Better To Travel

# *Better To Travel*

*Selected Poems*

Collin Kelley

To Blanche Babcock,
All good things!
Collin Kelley

iUniverse, Inc.
New York Lincoln Shanghai

**Better To Travel**
**Selected Poems**



iUniverse, Inc.

For information address:
iUniverse, Inc.
2021 Pine Lake Road, Suite 100
Lincoln, NE 68512
www.iuniverse.com

ISBN: 0-595-28409-4

Printed in the United States of America

For Christeen Snell

# *Contents*

## 1. The Passport On The Table

## 2. In Between Days



## 3. Sights Unseen

# *Acknowledgments*

This book would not have been possible without the support, input and feedback from these people: Tina Miller (sister, lifelong friend, heart), Malory Mibab, Joy Thomas, Grant Jerkins, Ferrol Sams, Robert Burch, Rose Hall, Joy Borazjani, Peter Kotowski, Jennifer Perry, the "Mothers Teresa"(Teresa Lyons and Teresa Yelverton Johnson), Merci Howe, Roslyn Targ, the Georgia Poetry Society, Chante Whitley-Head, Ginger Murchison, Kodac Harrison and the crew at Java Monkey Speaks, and my parents and family.

Special thanks to Ian Britton for his beautiful cover photograph taken in Northumbria in the United Kingdom. More thanks to Tina Miller for the photograph of me and to Elizabeth Holmes for her assistance in the graphic arts of this book.

For inspiration: Anne Sexton, Jane Siberry, Toni Morrison, Margaret Atwood, Laurie Anderson, Sharon Olds, Alice Walker, Wim Wenders, John Irving, Robert Frost, Rita Dove, Don DeLillo, Alice Walker, Sally Potter, Krzysztof Kieslowski, Adrienne Rich, Jeanette Winterson, Patricia Smith, Stan Rice Jane Campion and Kate Bush. Thank you.

Some of these poems have previously appeared in the following publications and online journals: *Welter, The Harrow, Sophomore Jinx, Offerings, Alternative Arts & Literature, lastwords.com* and *SubtleTea.com.* Other poems were part of two spoken word performances: *Poems for Conquering Venus,* which premiered on WREK's Advise and Dissent program, and *Two Voices.*

# 1. The Passport On The Table

## *Cool Retreat*

5:01 p.m. the day
after yesterday.
When you told me
over dinner you
would marry.
Of course, you never
noticed my sudden
loss of appetite.
I smiled and cooed
and ordered drink
number two.
I joked,
I'll be the best man,
but that was a lie.
If I were the best
man, you'd be
marrying me in June.
We are just friends,
on terms,
blotting out the bad
times...

your threatening hand,
your drug induced haze,

your inability to acknowledge
my compassion.

I wonder what kind of
man this must be,
who loves you enough
to commit.
What stamina does he
have that I lack?
How has he steeled
himself against your
petulance, your lack
of affection, your
irrevocable, damaging
words?

It must have been me.

Clever as ever,
I conceal my wound
and make a cool retreat
to sarcasm, other topics,
more wine.
I offer no satisfaction
if you're looking for a
crack in the armor.
That's all on the inside,
where you never bothered
to look.

Later that night,
the topic again,
I play if off, some

derisive shot over
your bow.

Will you give me away,
you ask.
I already have.

# *Firewater*

Back door, old house.
Snow melting faster
than paper burns.
And some child is
running in the woods.
He is at my side now.
Kissing my face,
holding my hands.
Bitterly cold, he
half naked.
I lead him to the
couch, lay him
down, smother him
with my body.
Kisses, apologies,
promises…forgotten.
Ghost.
He melts through my
veins like firewater.
And passes through my
soul as winter does.

# *The Gallows Coat*

Black folds ripple,
your coat on the door.
It hangs there still,
a modern day shroud
in appropriate color.
Resurrected from the
closet floor, a misshapen
mass of fibers.
I smoothed the sleeves
once filled by your
arms.
Pressed the cuffs that
collared fists.
Clenched or unclenched,
your hands were always
enraged.
I press the cloth close,
but never slip it on.
It is too large and consuming.
Pockets lined with old
delusions.
I make this door your
gallows and leave you
there to swing.

## *Baggage*

Last year,
the words,
unable to lift
my hand.
Paralyzed by inaction,
your non-reaction,
dissatisfaction.
I cannot rid my mind
of these thoughts
that cling like
a worn out scent on
a burnt out me.
Obsession redux,
living in flux.
Don't ask me questions.
The passport on the table
should be answer enough.
The house full of good-byes.
Everyday I mentally pack
my bags.
We are all full of impending
journeys.

# *Answering Machine*

You come home,
but things have changed.
If I could recall one sweet
memory, I'd share it with
you all.
But it escapes me now,
just as you did then.
When it took no effort
to pack and vacate
without notice.
I find you guilty of
desertion, but suspend
the sentence for time
served.
You move away, but
not on.
You call to announce
your imminent arrival,
as if I still care.
And then you leave
word of your new
address and the ominous
words that you're home
for good.
But I won't call, although
I'll carry the number at
all times.
Tucked between the card
that has just enough cash

to take me to Paris and the
ticket I saved to get to
town.
And I'll go without you,
and without a sound.
Consider me exiled,
expatriate, excommunicated.
It is just your voice on the
machine I could not face.
Start, stop, pause, erase.

# *Inertia (Belfast)*

Do not lie down,
is scrawled on the wall.
Would rather fall swiftly
and with blood.
Drag my body home
through the dark streets,
shut myself behind the
red door.
All at once I am inertia,
welcoming the floor.
Would rather be comforted
by carpet than rough hands.
The graffiti has many
meanings; I try to decipher
them all.
Do not crawl back to his
bed, do not look down
when reprimanded, do not
countenance staying here
forever.
One day I must pack my
rooms, as others have
done before me, and set
off for sights unseen.

# *Better To Travel*

The unused black
umbrella bit my
hand today.
Cheap, angry metal
and plastic offering
travel tips:
*Take me someplace*
*where it rains.*

# *London Underground*

Stand to the right
and mind the gap.
I watch from the
left and you slip
between the cracks.
There's no need to
dream here, we
are living one.
Sleep deprivation,
drunken laughter,
your stare reducing
me to ashes.
You're hiding behind
popularity and affected
aloofness.
It would be so easy
to let yourself go now.
No one would ever
know.
A city full of secrets
can handle one more.
It's your decision.
I know you know,
but refuse to see.
Walking the streets
of London, I am
distracted by my own
self-awareness.

# *St. Christopher's Place (London)*

7 a.m. heels click,
sounds like raindrops
or Nazis on the march.
Across the courtyard,
pretty blonde boys cut
hair, oblivious to our
stares and cares, wants
and needs.
It is the same day after
day.
Only we are different.
Only this room is in
constant motion,
transfiguration.
Tonight we would fill
it with smoke and jazz
if we had the way.
But instead we'll just
go to bed and prepare
for the sounds of morning.

## *The View From Here*

I watch for you at the window
that looks out on a small corner
of London.
I kneel in a chair, arms on dusty
sill.
At any moment, I'll see you for the
second it takes to cross the street.
My warm breath fogs the cool
glass where I write your name.
It is framed by the rooftops of
the city at late afternoon.
I have been here before, the
same pose, watching for you
and others who have and have
not come.
And for the little difference
it made, I'd hardly say it was
worth the wasted hours.
So what if you fill up the room,
you don't fill up me.
Furniture would suffice and
be a lot less trouble when the
corners need darkening.
Although I am not in love
with you, I probably could be
again.
If I could just find the beginning
of the time we shared together.
In some other life, there were

no interruptions or other people
in the way.
While you are out discovering
the places I already know,
I touch the places where you
have been.
Pull your discarded clothes to
my face, searching for the
essence that drew me to you
in the first place.

# *Envy (after The Portrait of A Lady)*

Her hand reaches for the door,
but she pauses and turns.
Freeze.
Like Isabel, I have been given
this choice in different seasons.
Flowering spring or cold winter,
two continents and happiness
fleeting on both.
I sat near you for three hours,
the hotness of your unwinding
body, the cologne, the Scotch
you had earlier.
These scents are my familiars
and I store them away for
future travels.
The streets of London are
filthy and I wonder how
something so massive could
ever be clean.
How will I ever rid myself
of the need to be needed by
anyone other than myself?
I distance myself from you,
but it feels like coldness,
and how do I make it thaw?

Last night, I was watched
for three hours by someone
more beautiful than you.

But I let the moment go.
Never uttered a word.
Disappeared into the streets,
never looked back.
A modern day Lot's wife
untempted by sin.

I admire the naiveté you
possess when it comes to
your looks.
Every head turns to watch
on crowded trains, but when
you look in the mirror you
are unsure.
Oh, to have that ignorance
of self.
Everyday I look in the mirror
and see exactly who is looking
back.
Maybe that is naiveté, too.

I would like Isabel's choices.
I would like to be the one
pausing at the winter door,
fully aware of past mistakes.
Knowing the future is in
my hands.
Freeze.

# *Come Back Unchanged*

Don't cut your hair,
lose weight, or buy
new clothes.
I want you just the way
I saw you the first time
on that London platform.

I think that I will always
look for you in crowded
theatres, in my peripheral
vision.
Your hand reaching to
push back stray hair, the
high color in your cheeks.

You'll be going home to
other arms, while my
house is dark and shuttered
for the season.
I would like to forget your
face, the little things that
make you whole.

And sometimes I am a
liar.
Your body is on top of me,
your hair falls in my face,
the early spring breeze
raises your flesh and I
study every bump, every

smooth place, every little
crevice like a map.
In my dreams, I will
retrace these steps, connect
the dots.
You wouldn't want to
confuse me by altering the
terrain.
Come back unchanged.

# *Unfurling*

Late at night, or not so late
depending on time zones,
when the pain behind my
eyes erupts like geysers,
I caress my head along the
sharp edges.
It brings me back into focus.
Love does not remain, but
my life remains before me.
Unfurling in slow motion
red flags, warning signals
to passing vessels.
Here is the snow I never
saw this season and the
great house I run towards.
If I go indoors does it mean
I cannot cope?
Will he or won't he reach
for the door?

The moon is too bright, a
midnight sun flooding my
room.
It falls across my pillow,
my eyes in highlight like
film noir, widened in terror.
Or is just overwhelming
awareness?
Sleep comes in slivers and

pierces just enough to dream.
I am haunted by the piano
and woodwinds and my
fingers resting so close to
your thigh.
You never felt them there,
but it was little jolts of
electricity here.
Bringing me to focus.
How did I ever let you slip
away?
Your fine skin and long dark
hair, the perfect hips.
We are in a theatre in
London, we are somewhere
together. How quickly I am
in that place that is nowhere
at all.
But there is the music, an
overture of things that have
come and gone.
I am hearing it right now
so clearly, my brain is the
instrument learning by
repetition.
All night I have hit repeat
and not grown tired of
the sound.
As I never grew tired of
you.

Somewhere it is snowing
and the moon is illuminating
the yard in harsh relief.
There are the footprints,
the winter grass showing
through, where someone
endlessly walks.
Haunted by music and
looking for something to
bring focus.
Somewhere there is a life
like mine unfurling in the
shadows.

## *Battersea*

We are riding out past
Battersea, the deserted
power station a hulking
relic.
Four smoke stacks against
grey dawn, waiting for
the sun.
This place looks better
in daylight, the glare hides
the decay.
This is the first and last
monument you see leaving
London by train.
Battersea is forbidding on
the way in, cause for
despair on the way out.
This morning, your profile
is framed by the window
as Battersea recedes.
As always, you remain an
enigma.
I know you so well, but
I am forever scratching
at the surface of the thing
we do not discuss.
Even exhaustion and
persistence can't crack
you open.

Why could you never love
me?

I acknowledge that we are
now over, that this trip is
a sort of closure four years
after the fact.
Why can't you say what I
already secretly fear:
I used you until I used you
up and gave nothing in
return.
This trip is your consolation
prize.
Be happy you're allowed
even this.
You say you are now
someone else, have
evolved.

On days like this, I'd like
to summon your old self
back and interrogate him
for hours.
Take a white hot light and
shine it in all the dark
places until they are bleached
and smooth.
No rough edges and easy to
read like a well designed
map.
But this won't happen today.

The sign says express, but the
train moves out like a funeral
procession.
Slowly passing Battersea as if
in memoriam.
The sun is not out.

# *Paris Hotel*

Somewhere beyond
this window is Paris.
For now, all I can do
is stare across
Rue Rampon.
I watch the old woman
tend her balcony full
of flowers, see inside
her spare rooms.
I chose to stay behind,
lying on the bed in
dark recess.
But I am thinking of
you.
The old woman sighs
and we hear the noises
of the city together.
She looks at me and
our eyes meet.
But she looks through
me, as if she's seen all
this before.

# *Simple Answers*

The simple answer is despair.
Paris left a scar.
Maybe it was the first day
there, exhausted and hating
the back of your head.
Or perhaps it was coming
from anything possible to
not a chance.
Underwater and speeding,
caution to the wind, a piece
of baggage left behind at
Waterloo.
At Gare du Nord, I almost
got back on the train to
London.
In reverse, back to the
other you.
I should have drowned
you in that pool.
It was the last good day.

Now I find my hands
clasped in prayer.
I hide behind locked
fingers as if they were
a mask.
They cover my eyes,
which hide nothing.
You never looked there

for answers.
There's no need to
understand me, you
say, accept this.

You fell asleep in the
Louvre and I consoled
myself with Mona Lisa.
She smiled back at me
through a barrier.
I know what you know,
her eyes seemed to say,
and it's safer behind the
glass.

## *Strings*

I see you on a street
in Berlin.
Reach out to touch
your tangled curls.
Walk through me.
I follow at a not so
discreet distance,
but I am unnoticed.
Although this is only
a dream, I understand
the strength of strings.
The one that holds you
high above and the one
that holds me back.
Would you pass me by
if I saw you today?
Smile thinly and turn
away?
As do all good strangers.
We all walk tightropes,
some higher than others.
I make this confession
without a net.
All angels wear armor.

# *The Level of Dreams*

Bare blue walls
is how I dream
your rooms, packed
for impending journey.
On one level, I see
far into the future.
This room full
again with books
and laughter.
On the next level,
the room is not
the same.
Subtle change of
shade and window
placement.
Your presence
more spectre than
spatial.
Later, someone I
identify as you
wears a scarlet
coat tied with a
sash.
We walk through
a park in Paris
and you have
transformed.
A mutation of all
those that came before.

They all wore red
at some point:
a badge of shame,
of delusion,
of danger.
This color says
run, but I wait at
ground zero like a
doomsday prophet.
Awake now and
exhausted.
Feeling the distance
breaking wide.
I turn over and you
are gone.

# *Fall Comes*

Wind under eaves,
threatens to lift roof.
Yesterday, I was too
introspective to write.
All the words turned
inside, ran circles.
My tricks and drop-off
dreams, unuseful.
I would write the day
upon a board, then
slowly rub it all away.
Clap off the eraser dust,
and fall to rest.
Goodnight, sweet you.
I light candles against
darkness instead.
Fire shimmer dances
in hidden drafts.
This storm will be
over by morning.
Artificial light reborn,
the bells and whistles
of everyday.
And all that will remain
is the convergence of
summer and fall.

Five months past,
again,
learning to crawl.

# *2. In Between Days*

## *Repentance*

10 p.m. you come down
the hall tapping out a
cancer stick.
A habit you promised
to break, but chose me
instead.
Three years ago Halloween
I went as a priest.
A costume I still wear
whenever we meet.
I feel the collar clutch
at my throat as we settle
into the box.
Begin absolution.
Push the wine this way,
mister.
The meat tastes bloody
in my mouth, like the
time you bit my tongue.
I could never eat properly
in your presence.
Too much effort to keep
up a crumbling façade.

I remember:
Shutter click on a Saturday

graveyard afternoon.
You Christ like and I some
second-rate magdalene.
I am the worst kind of whore,
because I would have you
here no matter the consequence.
I make room in the immortality
box, look at it sometimes,
cherish it never.
Those who are crucified don't
always rise from the dead.
I am a witness.

Why tell me these things now
when they no longer matter?
You said so yourself.
I am the repository of your
indiscretions.
Loan me some rebellion,
because I have pissed all
mine away.

*You are not my father.*

Mothers do rape their sons,
while Daddy blows up his
boyhood dreams in the backyard.
His occasional backhand is no
match for her nightly hand to
mouth.
The scars are the same.

You run away, but Daddy
doesn't understand why.

I remember:
Sitting in the middle of the
floor.
Tongue frozen, eyes rolling.
I can't stand to see you like
this.
So I don't.

*You are not my father.*

New Orleans was the last straw.
I thought the shit-stink streets
would ease my mind.
We, joined at hip and head,
a Siamese medusa.
Oh, me of forked tongue that
seeks your pleasure in two places.
But you fucked him anyway.
I watched from the eyes in the
back of my head.

I remember:
Lying here, refusing furniture
as comfort.
I chose the hard floor instead.
At least there was feeling.
Winter boards pressed against
my spine.

Any feeling will do, any
feeling at all.

*You are not my father.*

This is where I came in and
how we will go out.
I am not your father, but I
am the whore, the resurrection,
the jack in the box.
In the not so distant past,
you said these things were
enough.
Your repentance means nothing
to me, because I was trading
in sin long before you born.
At least in this, I will always
be one step ahead of you.

# *Diners at 2 a.m.*

Sometimes we do not speak.
For whatever reason:
Your mouth on mine,
our anger,
our separation,
fear,
loathing.

The silent tongues nurse
coffee at 2 a.m. in dirty
diners.
What crime committed?
Some new sin.
Back booth history:
little lies,
second chances,
thirds,
lasts,
good-byes.

Two years later,
on terms,
we seat ourselves.
Came in separate cars,
will go home to separate
houses.
In the formica confessional,
we still nurse our coffee.
Never speaking of past or

future, only in between.
You light a cigarette,
I stir the cream.

At 2 a.m. we sit next
to our ghosts, still locked
in combat.
And sometimes we do
not speak, because the
din of the past drowns
us out.

# *Night Working*

Your words run rings.
Sound of the telephone
2:30 a.m.
Not asleep, no.
I've stopped trying.
Work the dark shift,
brother, because you
don't prefer daylight.
I work the dark seam,
slipping in between
the dreams.
It is a middle ground
that knows no bounds
and leaves my waking
mind racing.
I lock the door and
crawl under my desk.
Await your next
transmission, confession.
There are so many things
not worth having, yet I
hold out my hand in
demand.
So many things left
unspoken, I would grow
extra ears for every last
whisper.
And Anne is there
above me, typing out

her dark words.
I lie against her
bruised legs, pray for
our healing.
Later, she'll swallow
the fumes and leave
me behind.
But don't take me
instead, I'll find my
way back to bed.
Someone has to keep
up appearances.

# *The Realization of Rain*

Make it rain
inside this room.
I see moving pictures,
grey screen,
dresses trailing in mud.
A distorted sound of thunder,
a muffled sound of falling rain,
in colorized meadows.
From every corner, shadows
inch like rising damp, running
down my face.
Rain is never ugly there,
even as it drowns the earth.
Press a hand against the
picture, all slick and flat.
Rain has a way of falling
inside your head, a constant
reminder.
It never rained a single day
you were here, now all it
does is pour.
Even in this picture room,
we watched the drops fall,
but on others a world away.
A shared fantasy of making
love in a storm.
Situations deteriorate rapidly,
water washing away the
beachhead.

The corrosion is soft and
steady.
One more memory in the
jar.
I can see it distorted and
bloated, like looking through
a teardrop.
When we speak of these days
of rain, we will mark a passage.
When I put my pen to paper,
nothing will smear out the words.
Days will pass into night,
unnoticed, with only clocks
to keep the difference.

# *Exhibit 1 (after viewing an exhibit by Henry Ossawa Tanner)*

Henry, did you know that freedom
was not a color on your palette?
In 1895 as the young man carved
in dark, muted shades.
In 1913 as the boat crossed raging
seas.
You mixed until your hands were
every color of the rainbow,
as every hand should be now and
then.
Henry painted through the era of
silence, the era of hangings.
His work lies in state.
Silent testimony, silent struggle.

# *Dreams (described)*

In dreams
the house is always
different and familiar
people wear the faces
of strangers.
I read unwritten books,
then forget the words
upon waking.
Other nights haunted
by people I barely
knew.
That girl I never spoke
to in the back row of
math class, that ugly
boy I never gave a
second thought.
Sometimes naked,
running from storms,
to arms, to chains.
Bound here night
after night, the only
choice is to play along.
So, I fall from countertops
in the strange house.
I kiss you again.

I seek shelter from the
bombs.
I spread my arms,
but never fly.

# *60 Seconds in Zaire*

Nestled between
the drive-by
shootings and
L.A. murder trials,
60 seconds in Zaire…

On the road,
human tidal wave.
Millions in flight,
deserting the homeland.

A child by the roadside,
surrounded by ruins.
The women cover their
mouths and noses.
Side-long glances, in
motion.

On a hillside in Goma,
50,000 or more.
City in temporary
standstill.
Hours for water, bread,
death.

A food line in Kibumba,
children scrambling for
fallen grain.

Some wear bowls as hats,
dreaming of water.

Genocide,
Cholera,
Typhus,
Death indiscriminate.

On hard molten ground
the bodies are lain.
Covered in dirt, mass
graves.
No words are said as
the bulldozers come.

In other news…

# *Short Time*

The sign says,
Will be back shortly.
When did you leave?
When will you come back?
How long is shortly?
We thrive on time,
and this is the gap.
A break in the flow.
Shortly is filled with
monsters under the bed,
deserting daddies,
distant sirens.
It is moments of truth,
waiting lines,
starving children,
a call from the doctor.
Shortly is vague and
ill defined, as all time
really is.
At least make it concrete,
for comfort's sake:
Will return at noon.
It's something to pin
your hopes on.
It's something to set
your watch by.

# *Red (for Judith)*

I dream the color
of your hair,
red and full of
regret.
I never told you
the truth.
My conscience
wears your face
as a reminder.
A backward,
mocking mask.

# *Machine as Intervention*

Twice this has happened.
I take it as a sign.
Bullshit scrolls and memory
chips wince.
I call for intervention from
some god, and my prayers
are answered.
I hit execute, but computer
baby has other ideas.
It processes my words into
oblivion, the empty index
a friendly reminder that
I can do better.

# *All Clocks*

All clocks are not
the same.
It's always some
waiting game.
One minute faster
on your wrist,
two on the TV,
five in the car.
Never spring
forward
wherever you are.
So what if I'm late,
love?
So what if my skin
is pale and the veins
are the hour hands
pulsing and winding
down?
I do not need your
fingers now.
Pressing my buttons,
real or imagined.
I prefer to be
maintenance free,
and keep up with
the race at my own
speed.

# *The Sickroom*

Life and death sit in
the sickroom,
brought forth from
the same womb,
a perfect set of twins.
Dare not name them.
Their separation is
only an illusion.
Invisible, but palpable.
A hot breath or cold
breeze on your neck.
The shiver they cause
is the thread of
existence that runs
through us all.

It must be the mother
who has died.
Pulled from the sickbed,
saying she was strong
enough to sit up,
knowing it would be
the final act before
lying down forever.
Father prays and the
children are frozen
or retreating to corners
or burying their faces.
Only one stares,

a woman, unblinking
into the maw of tomorrow
and the next day
and the next.

I have seen this before...
Three sisters after death,
gathering at the window
to watch the ocean that
yesterday swallowed
mother whole.
The tide rolls in and
takes away obligation
and leaves behind a
foam that is only fleeting
guilt.
This too, in time, will
be reclaimed.

Edvard stands in the door,
come to dissect the living
in funeral black, to make
time stand still.
One day that woman
will be you, he says.
It will be you who must
look up from the passing
and accept all the tomorrows.

I shiver,
and feel death stand up

and approach.
So tall and handsome.

And Edvard says, maybe
it is the twin.
Life coming to embrace
you, or maybe
his touch will be the cold
fingers of mortality.
Do you really want to
know the truth, shatter
the illusion?

So I walk with that tall
stranger.
Leaving the same way
I came in, entering the
room I had just left.
It is this close, life and
death.
Separated only by
connecting doors.
And the woman stares
at me with something
that resembles grief,
but I can only imagine
that it is sweet relief.

# *The Crash*

Things that could go
either way:
My phone list dropped
in the trash bin makes
me pause.
I could leave it there,
cast everyone off.
I'd have to wait for
the phone to ring.
There's some excitement
here, like the tingling
of approaching orgasm.

When I was fifteen, I
had a dream, wet and
exhausting, about wanting
to scream.
Not about some girl's tits
or some guy's dick, but
a non-working water
fountain and an upcoming
math test.
This combination of need,
anticipation and fear was a
blinding reality check.
I have never looked at a
water fountain the same
way again.
I dropped out of school

to avoid calculation,
yet I'm calculating my
every move, my every word,
the next action.

I kneel here by the trash bin,
the liner a startling white.
Silky and fresh.
Inviting me to take a chance.
And again there is that tingle,
coming on like car crash.
Some things are so unavoidable.
My hand moves…

The paper between two fingers
and I am overcome by anxiety
and exhilaration.
Two roads diverge into the
woods, neither of them well
traveled.
Today it could go either way,
I'd say.
The little things, the goddamn
little things.
I recall this waiting for the
phone to ring.
Contemplating white trash,
the motor crash and sticky
fingers.

# *Backstage*

In the half-light
you pull on your coat,
arm catches in sleeve.
I am there to free you.
Inside the cloth, I
feel the softness of
your skin against
the back of my hand.
An arm so smooth
it makes silk rough
by comparison.
Likewise your face,
so unblemished.
Only a bead of sweat
between your brow
mars the perfect
surface.
I touch that drop
with a fingertip, then
slowly trace the
curves of your face.
My whole hand
searching for lines
that don't yet exist.
When my palm brushes
your mouth, I feel
your lips kiss the inside.
We do this in semi-
darkness until you

are summoned away.
Light shows every
irregularity.
I see better in the dark.
Have just seen you
in a way no one else
ever will.
You say this does not
matter, that it was a
momentary lapse of
reason.
Darkness, sometimes,
makes us do unexplainable
things.

# *The Advent of Rage*

The dropping of keys,
thousand yard stares,
traffic delays and
falling down stairs.
It is the coming of
rage without measure
Burn you down with
one match, immolate
myself with another.
Death is only worth
a column inch, and
someone else is in
charge.
They can send you
out in style or bury
you under probate.
It's the little things,
the goddamn little
things, that make
me homicidal.
The tone of your
voice, pop songs by
sixteen year olds,
politicians, pro-lifers,
racists and homophobes.
The list is endless
You could go back and
forth to the moon twice
on the fuel of my rage.

But it goes both ways.
Because on the other
side of that peaceful
picket fence are people
who plan assassinations
of saints, pollute the air,
violate no-fly zones,
bomb motorways,
commit genocide.

*I like you, do you like me?*
*Check yes or no.*

*I hate you, do you love me?*
*Check…*

*I love you, do you hate me?*
*Check…*

The advent of rage begins
here, a children's game.
Rejection from the mouths
of babes escalates over time.
It adds up to a price we all
must pay.
This is the sum of us.

## *Progress*

Things that unwind
over time, make me
stop short and stare.
You are four years
gone, yet your face
appears in the most
unexpected places
and the most
inopportune times.
As in life, so are you
in death.
I still chill to the
bone trying to find
balance with your
lifeless body.
I watched you age
over years and now
your picture hangs
on my wall—a modern
day Dorian Gray.
Most days I look in
the mirror expecting
to find that pristine
seventeen year old I
used to be, something
else dead and gone.
I wonder if you would
like me this way?
In the picture,

you are draped over
a chair, eyes averted,
fingers locked.
Your jacket is half on,
half off and this disturbs
me more than I can say.
Like you gave up years
earlier, the effort to
dress or undress already
too much a burden.
Some days I find myself
sitting in a chair, my
jacket half on, half off.
I finally let it fall to the
floor.
At least this is some kind
of progress.
Some movement toward
decisiveness you never
had.

# *The Mask (for B.D.)*

This is a dream of falling
overboard.
Finding yourself under the
surface and navigating
strange waters.
Down here is the intricate
puzzle, where the pieces
don't always lock.
Or else it is connect the
dots.
What will the picture be
at completion?
Sometimes I shudder at
the emerging image.
In the beginning, like
all strangers, you are a
dark faraway thing.
Blurring at the edges,
maybe dangerous.
Then your mouth makes
contact with mine so
unexpectedly.
It is brief, but it is soft
and unlocks doors.
Part of the mystery rises
to the top, even as it goes
deeper.
I have always been one
for the game—the give and

take, the licking of wounds,
the hard won victories.
Sometimes it is just better
this way, the losses easier
to forget.
But I must admit,
on rainy afternoons I dream
of painting your mouth
scarlet and then kissing
it all away.
Would wear it like a badge
until the fade.
All moments of pleasure
eventually do.
So if you often find me
staring, it is just that I am
looking at your eyes.
These things are anchors,
they are portals,
for those of us who dream
of exploring further
below the surface.

# *The Gift (for Diana)*

Your face is a fan
spread out before me
just as it has been, one
way or another, for the
last sixteen years.
I have been an
unfaithful lover.

I adored your shimmering
skirt, your feline face
with upturned eyes under
bangs.
I coveted your image, the
sweet femininity, the
fairy tale.
I was your devoted slave
at 4 a.m., exhausted and
elated.
I secretly wished you
had married me instead.
It was one of the last best
years.
I remember being twelve
and having this terrible
crush.
But it went away, as all
crushes do.

Packed away in a box
for future remembrances.

For two days after your
death, I searched desperately
for these things,
the artifacts,
overcome with the irrational
thought that if I couldn't
find them all would be lost.
But you are lost.

Now I have them, all
yellowed clippings and
dog-eared books.
On my lap are the pictures
of my childhood.
You are still nineteen and
the innocence radiates, but
in 1981 I had no concept.
We were both still untouched,
unscarred.
But I know you were not
that in the end, and I know I
will not be when I die.

The house is full of candles
now, because any other light
seems unnatural.
I have collected more images
of you in death than I ever
owned in life.

I pour over your face,
marking passages,
seeking out lost time.
I never knew you, never met
you, sometimes never gave
you a second thought.
But I am you.
We all are in some way.
Living and dying in a light
less luminous, hidden in
plain sight.
What you craved most.
It's such a simple thing,
the only gift I would have
offered.

The bell tolls every minute
and half way around the world,
the darkness gives way to dawn.

## *Ice Storm*

The front door is
off its hinges,
re-latching a losing
battle.
You've come to me
three times, your
chest puffed out
like a man with a
smile that betrays
the boy that lingers.
The rain splatters
the window as if
attacking.
Drawn to my face
like a magnet.
I draw your memory
this way.
Alternately saving
my life and leaving
me to die.
And you are always
fucking, but never me.
Your promises of
sex like a summer
primary, easily
forgotten in the fall.
With devotion
secured, you fled
north to a cold climate.

Packing up your
ice pick mind, you
thought you were so
sharp.
A prick, yes, but
never deep enough.
Never satisfying.
Here I am with blood
on my legs and your
arms wrapped around
me.
I am dying, but you
are grace.
Here is the circus,
where you whisper
those entreating words.
I am masturbating on
the floor, you watch
me like a documentary.
In pictures and dreams,
you are the ice storm
I could never escape.
It is ten years now and
I am still waiting for
the thaw.

# *Water (remembered)*

I came to collect the prize
one month after your marriage.
Standing on the same rocks,
unnatural beachhead to save
disappearing shore.
I remember the water pounding
the black stone, rising up to
sink the pier.
See the water stain wet where
the tide rolls back to reveal
stairs.
I dream I am a woman in
wedding white walking,
my dress soaking up the sea
like a sponge as I descend
the steps.
The fabric once so light and
full of air becomes the black
weight that will pull me under.

There was always water
where you were concerned.
Tears and rainstorms,
car accidents spilling fluid
on blacktop.
Our last night was a harbinger
of this future shock, when the
storm moved in and the lights
went out.

I am in a car on a side street
stripping off uncomfortable
clothes and the pavement
reflects like glass.
People walk by en route to
the party, see me nearly
naked in this wet box.
And it thrills me, but not
like you.

I remember the day you told
me to buy the most expensive
thing because I couldn't live
without it.
And I still can't.
I have amassed a fortune of
goods on your words.
Telling me in your subtle
way that you were not for
sale.
I am still searching for your
limit.
Everyone has a price.

And I have pinpointed the
moment when everything
came undone.
When a single word would
have sufficed and cracked
you open.
You are young and mute
sitting in the car looking

out the window.
Anywhere but at me,
because I am the mirror.
I am clutching the wheel
in a death grip, waiting for
impact.
If you had turned then,
if I had pulled over,
if our eyes had met,
at least I would have been
sure.
Could have moved into
middle age with peace
of mind.
Now we are ten years
removed and your intentions
are still as incalculable as
they were that night.

Many strangers have touched
me in the elapse of time.
I have courted others that
contain your trace elements,
hoping to divine the loss,
wishing for them to channel.
We speak in tongues and
teeth and overheated backseats.
Nothing rubs off.
They are not from your mold.

I learn of your marriage months
after the fact, sitting at my desk

minding my own business.
The ocean rushes back, the tide
threatens to overtake me.
It is November and I was
collecting a prize that wasn't
you.
Even then, the power of the
water made me step back.

# 3. Sights Unseen

## *Things Change*

Mind races, out of control.
I thrash under the bedclothes
at 3 a.m.
Some paranoid army marching
in my brain.
It is the same scene, second
after second.
Fight and fall back.
I am shot, I die.
Or it shifts to something
more disturbing.
You again, slow motion.
Slipping away from me
over and over.
The bed soaked in sweat,
I am drowning myself.
I try to slip away.
I tear the house down
looking for pills.
To put me cool at ease.
There is one left in a bottle
at the back of the drawer.
It is enough for now.
Death for eight hours,
resurrection tomorrow.

I may feel differently.
Things change.

## *One Year*

In this dream you return
in an indefinable blackness.
Your white skin a beacon,
coming fast,
hands displacing water.
I wake without answers,
we all do,
one year later.
What you have touched in
me will never quite heal.
I know there are others,
sitting in dark rooms,
lighting candles, writing
words like these.
You have crept in,
made us your blood
memorials.
Send us subconscious
signals, your refusal to
be put in a drawer.

And these are my own
hands.
They hang mute at my
side, improper instruments
to define how I feel.
And your face is everywhere
still, but it is frozen in time.
We have built you a temple

of ascension and yet you
do not rise.
These hands are only good
for holding you down, it
is a collective effort.
How do you let go of a
perfect thing knowing
there will be never be
another?
It is the coveted childhood
toy your parents would
not buy, not giving in to
the whims and cries.
It remains a haunting
image of things lost.
You have become that
thing, my girl, and you
are just as unobtainable.

In this dream I build a
time machine, retrace
your steps, break the
cycle.
I call your name, you
look up, a split second.
Make myself an accomplice
in cheating unacceptable
fate.

## *Wired World*

I have become one
with the underworld,
sitting in front of a
flat screen, illuminated
by bruised light.
My fingers move over
keys, but play a different
tune.
A silent song that reaches
into the night, connects
on a million levels over
a trillion lines.
We are headed for
uncertain times
and some days feel like
last gasps.
I talk to boys who need
me sight unseen.
I want something that
leaves a taste in my mouth
and that burns.
Call me old fashioned.

These words that fly through
the air are not enough, yet
they have ruled my world
for so many days, making the
very pen I hold obsolete.
But tonight at 1:30 a.m. the

empty paper glowed in the
dark, demanded an accounting
for all the wordless days and
gathering dust.
Can't you see I'm only
traveling a wired world?
It calls me to action as it
threatens to leave me behind.
Even now it is changing.
Like some sci-fi fantasy,
the machine takes life.
It feeds off the
lonely hearts,
the pornographers,
the scientists,
the suicides,
the media,
the wars,
the stock market.
It is a colony teaming with
ants feeding an unknown
queen.
The world is recreated
daily.
We take this box and fill
it with past imperfect and
future despair.
We whisper to it our
hopes and dreams in quiet
little clicks.
One day it will just be

another mirror.
A mundane, every day
thing we only occasionally
contemplate at the best
and worst of times.
It can be and will be dust
one day.
Everything returns.
Tonight, I'll make myself
turn off the world.

# *Another Country*

Tempt with your pretty face,
your smooth belly,
your sordid past.
These things attract and
repel at will, and I cannot
sit still.
You are dancing and
showing too much to
strangers.
Old habits hard to break.
I find myself filling in
your missing hours,
wondering how you
mark time and with who.
I am not out of your
league, just off-world.
I have come home from
London, but find myself
still in another country.
Third world, still
developing.
London doesn't seem so
foreign anymore, only
it has a better selection
of music and magazines
to fill the void.
But the need to start
again remains, that need
for upheaval.

I step off the plane and
find myself in a too
familiar place.
Summer is coming.
I am unprepared.

# *Loss of Sense Memory*

I watch old memories unspool
in ragged, jarring images.
Untrained camera man, tourist,
shootist.
I was in your sights once, but
now I have no memory.
In an airport on the way to
New Orleans, pausing outside
Buckingham Palace
(we can walk, it's not that far).
There I am, and there you are, but
it is like watching someone else.
An observation dream state, third
person.
I was there; I have souvenirs
and a diary to keep the days.
We are in a red phone box on
Birdcage Walk, packed in like
circus clowns in tiny cars, breath
fogging the window.
Did it really happen this way,
mugging and laughing? I watch
now in something like awe, sifting
my brain like a gold miner for
nuggets.
I make jokes about airplanes
crashing, when it was appropriate
and not cause for frowns.
And then the image shifts and the

marksman catches me off guard,
between the seats on the Gatwick
train.
You and I contemplating departure,
the long good-bye that had been
four years coming.
We would never be this close
again.
I am told this is sense memory
loss. The brain packing away
the past, the unnecessary, and
leaving just a synopsis.
It is like reading a dust jacket:
enough to recall the story,
but the emotions, the details,
never surface.
One day, this will be the story
of our lives.

# *New York*

I have been to New York.
Flew over the giant crater,
but did not get close up.
On a terrace 21 stories high,
I saw the gap in the skyline.
Almost as if those towers
had been the head of a long,
lean body.
Now it is decapitated, now
it is empty shoulders that
somehow must remain
strong.
The hole beckoned me, the
sound of machinery, the
rustle of disintegrating
paper and fading lost faces,
tacked to fences and light
poles.
"My son's name is…,
he was in Tower Number
One."
Every road seems to lead
south into a heart of
darkness that will never
be defined.

There were policemen at
every block.
It was a feeling of both safety

and portent.
The t-shirts said,
I Still Love New York,
but the heart that pumped the
life blood still hemorrhaged.
Wounds do heal, but not yet.
Not when I can still see the
planes approaching, not when
I can see the bodies falling,
not when that spire slips into
a sea of smoke and ashes.
I watched it happen a thousand
miles away, but it tore through
me like 3,000 knives.
As if every soul clawed at the
living for one last breath of
life.

And I try to banish it all from
my mind, sick of hearing about
this un-winnable war on terror.
As long as there are divisions
in race, in religion, in politics,
over parcels of land, there will
always be terror.
We can drop bombs from dusk
till dawn, but evil is not so
easily vanquished.
Just ask God and the Devil.
Or simply ask the Israelis and
Palestinians if the war on terror

is being won as suicide bombers
strike weekly and make back
page news.
You can blur dividing lines, but
divided minds are something
else.
Those filled with a clear,
crystalline idea of destruction
are often missed by air strikes.

I don't watch the talking heads
at night.
Would rather stare at the dark
walls.
But even then the reel unfurls.
I cannot tear myself away from
those September images.
They play over and over in my
head like a broken record, the
needle sticks in the groove and
circles, and circles and circles.
I am still learning not to lose
sleep.

# *Tapestry*

Black sister touch my skin.
My boy waits at home, his
warm Asian hands make my
world go round.
White woman, original
mother, speak to me of
Virginia Woolf.
Indian girl lead me to the
river and bless me for I
have sinned.
Arab man wrap my hair
in your long white veil
and show me the sand.
Jewish father, sprinkle
me with ancient wisdom.
Spanish lover whisper
in my ear the secret of
Virgin Mary.
All you natives, bring me
to my knees and show
me the whole world.
Give me your history
lesson, your strange fruit,
your trail of tears, your
picket lines, and water
cannons, your
immigration, and
expatriation.
Lead me through war

and division, through
Selma, Lord, Selma and
Stonewall.
To Belfast and the
streets of Baghdad, to
the West Bank and
110 floors in mirror
flame.
Fill me with grace,
all you lifesavers.
Come out of the storm
and into the boat.
We rock on the waves
as one.
We look beyond the
bombs and the warmongers
call.
We disarm or die.
Come to my bed, every man
and every woman.
Tell me all your secrets, your
hopes and fears.
Weave me a tapestry of
one true thing. Sing me a
Song of Solomon…
Your left hand under my
head, your right hand
embrace me.
We spin like a top in
infinity, this little upside
down world.

I would ask for peace and
understanding, but these
words never translate
across oceans.
If everything could be still
for just one moment, with
illness, hunger and hate on
holiday, then we could see
that indefinable dream.
We could invent new words
for silence and hope.
Move with me, rock with me,
all you lifesavers.

# *Joint Decision (for Frida Kahlo)*

Me and Myself sit on
a bench with our hearts
in our hands.
Blood drips on white,
scissors flash red
and silver.
Pin that pulsing mass
to our sleeves.
Take a good look.
Your lack of observation
calls for extreme
measures.
All you see is surface:
the hole in our chests,
the imperfect butchery.
It is inside, beyond the
obvious, where the
intricate damage has
been done.
Even before, when we
were whole, you never
saw past the outer shell
and the fact that I
divided to meet
your never-ending needs.
But we both took a poll,
joined forces,
held each others hand
as the knife made entry.

Would rather cut out
our own than have it
ripped by your ignorance.
In this action we are one.
Unified in decision,
unmoved by your wants.

# *Weather Storm*

I meet your twin on a cold
Saturday afternoon,
he comes into the room
unaware, just as you did
then.
Doppelganger, hologram,
replicant.
He is your very essence at
seventeen, before you were
laid low by your uncontrollable,
unconscionable needs.
His smooth face, perfect
blonde hair, languid body
language.
At once aloof and laser
focused, one glance is
enough to prompt time
travel.
I invent scenarios both
sexual and benign, put us
there like puppets and
manipulate the strings
Then I realize that this is
misplaced desire.
I have already had you
and it laid me low, brought
me to my knees like a
slave at the whip.
And so you pass through

like a storm front,
raging over my head and
heart for two days.
I thought I would have to
seek shelter, but I weathered
you.
Without an umbrella, without
tears, without a sound but
these words.

## *Resurfacing*

For two months,
in darkness,
I bled myself
clean of you.
Leeched you out
in a warm bath,
watched you
swirl away.
Emaciated,
famine delirium,
I cured myself
of hunger.
Rearranged the
rooms to confuse
the past.
One night,
waking in cold
sweat and tears,
fever broken.
Resurfacing.

# *Arrivals and Departures*

The danger is not departing,
but arriving.
When you step into the crush
of kissing hands and contorted
faces.
By boat or plane, you must
descend and shake of yesterday's
cowl and slip on tomorrow's
coat.
Two sizes too small, but aren't
we all, when facing the unknown.
I prefer not to meet you at gates
or platforms or terminals.
In dreams, trains always mean
transition, possibly departure.
No matter where you go,
you're always leaving, even
as you arrive.
Destinations are nothing but
numbers kept by unfaithful
clocks.
It's what is beyond Victoria's
bustling floor that calls.
Something more than doors
and walls.
Until you hit the teeming
streets, you're never really
there.
So, square your shoulders

for what you have to do.
Until you've made the
decision to stay,
you're only passing through.

# *Sights Unseen*

Leaving now,
again,
always.
I dream of
constant
motion,
of not coming
home.
Nomad,
persona non grata,
unleashed.
Answer to no
one but myself,
meet questions
head on.
Cut ties,
lifelines,
comfort zones.
Future sight:
a low brick
house near the
Outback.
Open arms,
that embrace
and let go
easily.
Simple room,
life,
uncomplicated.

Going now,
fast forward,
disembodied.
Not just one
place, but all
sights unseen.
Waiting for the
corporeal to
follow.

www.collinkelley.com

Visit Collin Kelley's Official Poetry Website for new works, upcoming appearances, events and Kelley's monthly column.

E-mail: collinkelley@hotmail.com

0-595-28409-4